My Child, My Friend

Emotional Survival Skills for LDS Mothers

Dorothy L. Nielsen & Claudia Nielsen Evans

The inspiration for this book comes from Ezra Taft Benson's speech "To the Mothers in Zion," 22 February 1987. Quotations are from the brochure published Salt Lake City, UT: Church of Jesus Christ of Latter-day Saints, 1987.

© 1990 Covenant Communications, Inc.
All Rights Reserved
Printed in the United States of America
Library of Congress Catalog Number 90-080569
Dorothy L. Nielsen & Claudia Nielsen Evans
My Child, My Friend
Printed March 1990
ISBN 1-555-03-273-7

Dedicated to our children, Tamera, Kristen, Kate, Stan, Clarice, Elden, Rachel and Thomas who have allowed themselves to be seen as imperfect people struggling with imperfect mothers.

Notes from Our Children

During the process of work on our book, our children made comments that we have laughed about and learned from. Tamera said, "When I was growing up, I'm glad nobody ever told me I was supposed to hate my mother—I never felt the need to—still don't." Kristen remarked, "Tell anything you want about me in your book, Mom, if you think it will help another mother. I know YOU needed all the help you could get!" Kate commented modestly, "It's okay to let your humanity hang out, Mom. You weren't perfect, but look how splendidly I turned out!" Stan said, "Way to go, Mom—you can thank me for providing enough information for several volumes!"

Clarice, awed with the project, and showing that deeper understanding all mothers hope for, said, "I have known you, Mom, for almost twenty years now, and yet I am just beginning to recognize the depth and breadth of your strength. I honor, love, and adore you." Elden remarked, "I think you get more kicks out of writing about how to be a good mother than you do in being one." When Claudia asked Rachel how she liked her book, Rachel replied, "I love everything you make me, even if its just Cheerios." Thomas made the most candid conclusion, "I hope you're not going to tell everything you do in that book of yours because nobody will read it!"

When Claudia, Dorothy's oldest daughter faxed final changes to Darla, she added a note: "P.S. Fax my deepest love to my co-author and friend, Mom." Writing the book was an exercise in all it teaches!

Acknowledgements

Writing this book has been another evidence to us that "no man is an island; no man stands alone." We have shared the experiences and thinking of many mothers who have contributed their stories to make this book possible.

We acknowledge the thoughtful guidance of our editor, Darla Hanks Isackson, who helped us conceive the idea for the book, nourished us through nine months of incubation, and rejoiced with us upon delivery.

Thanks also to Laurie Nabozny who retyped and rearranged ad infinitum, and always arranged to do it with a smile.

To Kenneth Hennefer, clinical psychologist and friend, we pay special tribute. He has carefully taught our family how to parent and survive. We have graduated from his parental reform school without complete burn-out or casualty. . .yet.

Most gratefully, we give thanks to the Prophet, Ezra Taft Benson, who admonished us to "do things together". Writing this book has encompassed listening, praising, laughing and crying together. It is a testimony that working together on a project affords the kind of sharing that friendship is all about.

Our final thanks to our husbands, Talmage and Tom, for their constant encouragement and undying confidence in us and the children.

Table
of
Contents

Introduction

*P*resident Ezra Taft Benson, in his landmark address "To the Mothers in Zion," 22 February 1987, made this plea, "Mothers, take time to be a real friend to your children. Listen to your children, really listen. Talk with them, laugh and joke with them, sing with them, play with them, cry with them, hug them, honestly praise them. Yes, regularly spend unrushed one-on-one time with each child. Be a real friend to your children". (p. 8).

As mothers, we all long to build the kind of friendships with our children that President Benson encouraged. But we don't always know how. The purpose of this book is to provide practical answers to the question, "How can I be a friend to my children?"

While trying to build meaningful relationships with our children, we may feel as if we're paddling upstream in a leaky boat with a set of splintered oars. Perhaps this is true because we haven't yet learned some of the survival skills that will help us to paddle smarter, instead of harder. When the tempest is raging, we need lifelines to anchor us in the storm, and we need them before we exhaust ourselves beating against the waves.

We know how mothers have suffered when their relationships with their children have been damaged, because we have been there. This book has been created for mothers everywhere who want to learn new, creative ways to build friendships with their children. As co-authors, both of us have done extensive research and surveyed more than 200 mothers, gathering ideas and stories. Mark Twain once advised, "Get your facts first, and then you can distort them as much as you please." (*From C To C, Letter #37.*) In this book, we have altered the facts only to clarify a point or to protect the dignity of a person. To share individual experiences, as well as the principles that we jointly believe in, we also identify ourselves when we give a personal example. We alternate masculine and feminine pronouns in referring to our children.

What we aimed for was an easy-to-read, easy-to-apply, do-it-on-the-run, handy guide of the most essential principles of relationships. We are vividly aware that these ideas—even though perfectly understood and perfectly used (which is a perfect impossibility!)—do not assure perfect results. We need to avoid the unrealistic expectations and overzealousness that may keep us from seeing and appreciating our sincere efforts and genuine progress toward better relationships. Elder Howard W. Hunter assures us:

> A successful parent is one who has loved, one who has sacrificed, one who has cared for, taught, and ministered to the needs of a child. If you have done all of these and your child is still wayward, or troublesome, or worldly, it could well be that you are, nevertheless, a successful parent. Perhaps there are children who have come into the world who would challenge any parent under any circumstances. Likewise, perhaps there are others who bless the lives of, and are a joy to, almost any mother. (*Ensign, Nov. 1983, p. 65*)

In our own mothering efforts, we have struggled, failed, and learned valuable lessons that have helped us to avoid remaking the same mistakes. As a mother-daughter team, we have formed a fast friendship that motivates us to share these friendship-building principles with you. We want this book to be, in fact, a mother's answer to a prophet's plea.

Turning Points

We are all imperfect mothers. There are times when the tasks of mothering leave us overwhelmed and panicky. Claudia remembers: My bright, nineteen-year-old son, Elden, had such polished debating skills that he could argue with an echo and win. One day when he was about six, I recall struggling for unimpeachable answers to his probing question, "What is the position of the Church on dinosaurs?" Later, catching me on the rebound, my nine-year-old Thomas queried, "Are the star constellations moving with the earth or are they moving with the earth's galaxy?" Often, I've felt that the mothering process has not only used my education, but has outrun it, and sent me searching for answers in a million different ways.

Dorothy remembers feeling unappreciated, unaccepted and incompetent as a mother when a daughter left home and demanded more emotional space. She says: My beautiful, gifted daughter and I had been growing further and further apart for some time. Now she was in her early twenties, established in her own apartment, surrounded by her own friends, and seemingly without room for me in her life. I thought long and prepared prayerfully before I drove up to her apartment. I rang the bell, trembling. Her welcome was not warm. She pulled away from my embrace.

"Could I come in?" I asked, my chin quivering. "I've come to mend fences."

"It's too late, Mom, you should have tried *that* a long time ago."

"I realize that now, but I didn't know how to do it a long time ago.

3

But today I think I do, and I have come to ask you to forgive me and be my friend," I said earnestly. I felt tears stinging my eyes.

Grudgingly she asked me to come in and sit down. "But I don't want to be your friend," she said bluntly. "You've done too many things to hurt me. I can never forget them and *never* mend fences with you."

"I'm sure I've hurt you in ways I never intended nor realized," I admitted.

"Yeah, you have. You pushed me to do all the right things, but you were never there when I needed you. I can't remember *once* when you came into my room, sat on my bed, asked me how my life was going, and even tried to be my friend. So why are you suddenly trying now?"

"Because I realize the mistakes I've made." Then after a long pause... "and because I love you."

"Go tell that to somebody else because I don't believe you. How could you love a person who never did anything right? I had the wrong friends. I wore the wrong clothes to the wrong movies. I had the wrong opinions. I wore the wrong makeup and the wrong hairstyle. I did *everything* wrong! That's the way you made me feel," she burst out bitterly.

I listened for a long time as she spewed out her hurt and anger. "I'm guilty," I confessed at last with tears. "I *was* not and *am* not a perfect mother. I would like to have been better. I tried. I tried too hard. I wanted to do and say the right things that would bind us together in love, but I didn't always know what to say and how to say it, nor what to do and how to do it." I stroked her arm as we sat side by side on the sofa and could feel the stiffening of her body ease into relaxation as I held her hand between mine.

She kept talking. I kept listening. Finally, after I heard her out, she slumped, emotionally exhausted, into my arms.

"I don't care so much where we have been in our relationship as where we're going," I said soothingly. "I'd like to erase the dark spots and start writing in more bright ones. I'm beginning tonight. I've come to say I'm sorry. I want to be your friend."

"But I've told you, I don't want to be yours, Mom," she said firmly as she moved out of my arms, not allowing the softening that I could feel break through her wounded heart. "It's simply too late."

"It's not too late for me," I replied, as she walked behind me to the door. "But I honor your feelings. If you ever change your mind, remember that my heart is full of love, and my arms are open and ready to receive you."

She did not answer me as I stepped out of the unlighted doorway. She did not snap on the porch light or ask me to come again. I was crying. As I stumbled down the dark stairs, I remembered some of the other times I had stumbled in the mothering process. I had driven my children unmercifully toward perfection, lecturing, advising, and moralizing over hundreds of values. I had created unrealistic expectations for myself as well as my children.

Still, I walked to my car determined that I would not lose all sense of patience and charity toward myself. I had come. I had listened. I had not blamed or accused. I had not lashed back in anger. Certainly, I would not give up on my efforts to rebuild a friendship with my daughter. What had gone wrong in the past or even tonight was not necessarily the final chapter in our relationship. After all, I had not failed unless I stopped trying.

Our relationship had been breaking down for years. I knew it would take years to rebuild. It has. But we're both growing— growing up and growing closer together and appreciating each other as separate and different. I no longer feel desperate and depressed about it. I sincerely love and respect who she is and celebrate her individuality and abilities. I honor her!

We mothers sometimes think it's our sacred duty to not only bring our children up but to shape them up as well. We desperately want to help them avoid the pitfalls of life, and we feel we have the answers—all the answers—in gospel principles. And we do. However, we've learned through sad experience that using these principles as a stick to beat our children with usually doesn't squelch their undesirable behavior, but may destroy our friendship with them.

If the relationship is damaged, our children won't listen to gospel principles, no matter how diligent our efforts may be. The most effective way to really "shape up" our children is to genuinely befriend them, letting them know that they are more important to us than *any* principle. This is the attitude behind unconditional love. It says, "Our relationship is more important to me than the length of your hair, the style of your clothes, or the beat of your music. Our mutual respect and friendship is supremely important to me because I love you." Only when our relationship is intact, are we in a position to influence our children to internalize principles.

Elder Jack H. Goaslind reminds us, "None of us does everything right all the time. We are in the process of perfection. Just as there are no perfect children, there are no perfect parents—not in this life at least " (Church News, Feb. 28, 1987, P. 3).

Our children certainly know how it feels to have imperfect mothers! Because we have often tried too hard to make every worthy gospel principle a part of their lives, we have sometimes pushed principles and standards so unrelentingly that our friendships have suffered. In order to rebuild those friendships, we had to learn a foreign language—the language of unconditional love. Yet that language was not so strange after all. As we fumbled to learn it, we recognized that it was the love the Savior has always extended toward us. With new insight and inspiration, we determined to rescue broken relationships. The methods and principles and ideas we learned in that process are summarized in this book.

Listen Heart to Heart

"Listen to your children, really listen."
—President Ezra Taft Benson

Making friends with our children includes the ability to listen heart to heart. Such listening encourages sharing and builds trust. It creates an emotional climate that allows our children to come to know the deep and shallow places in their own souls.

Claudia says: My four-year-old Thomas came to me fairly bursting with concerns. I listened absently, continually interjecting my own thoughts. Finally, the little boy reached the point of exasperation. Clenching his fists and stiffening his elbows, he exploded, "Mom, will you stop erupting me! I'm trying to tell you something!"

Frequently, it's difficult for us to listen to the souls of our children when our own thoughts are "erupting" so loudly. Further, it's difficult to listen when the dishes are clattering or the vacuum is roaring or the printer is churning out paper. Building friendships with our children involves both an uncluttered mind and a receptive spirit. It asks us to give undivided attention when it is needed, using eye-to-eye contact and heart-to-heart communication. It also includes an honest appreciation of the worth of each child, who is also a child of God and heir to His qualities. Children can feel this regard. By an understanding tone of voice, an empathetic look on the face, and a loving expression in the eye, we communicate to the child that his feelings are important. We encourage him to get in touch with those feelings and express them, appropriately and honestly.

In a functional family, all members are able to express feelings.

In a dysfunctional one, parents and children deny their feelings and/or express them inappropriately.

Roadblocks to Understanding

To help our children know of our respect for them, we need to regard any feeling expressed—whether positive or negative—as valid. If we take up residence inside a child's point of view and listen for understanding, she will be able to tell the consideration we have for her feelings and be encouraged to keep talking. But if we deny the feeling or attempt to argue it away with such expressions as "You shouldn't feel that way" or "It couldn't be all that bad," communication will probably shut down. Here are some examples:

> Sue (age thirteen): I hate Jackie. She hangs around and clings to me like glue. She's always begging something off me, and she looks so scrubby.
>
> Mother: You shouldn't feel that way, honey. Jackie comes from a good family and she needs your friendship. Maybe you can help her.

We often disapprovingly try to talk our children out of their feelings and give unsolicited advice. This is a perfect trap for LDS mothers. Teaching moments are important to us, but we misuse them if we try to give a Sunday School lesson instead of a listening ear.

In response to Jackie's statement, this mother might keep Jackie talking and get a better understanding of her feelings with one of these approaches:

> You don't like someone latching onto you.

> It's uncomfortable having a person invade your privacy.

> With her sticking around you, you don't feel free to go where you want to go and do what you want to do.

It isn't fun to be glued to a slouch or a moocher.

Then Jackie could respond without defensiveness:

> Jackie: You got it! I feel stuck, trapped.
> Mother: That's not a good feeling.
> Jackie: It sure isn't!

> (As Mother listens, Jackie may begin to solve her own problem.)
> Jackie: But I know I shouldn't be mean to her. Her mom always treats me nice.
> Mother: See what you can do; but if you want to talk about some ways of easing out of it, let me know and I'll think through some with you.

Next are examples with an eight-year-old son, then a ten-year old daughter:

> Jed: Nathan won't let me play with his new battery-powered constructs. He won't let me play with his old ones either. He's such a selfish pig. He hogs everything.
> Mother: I'm surprised! You shouldn't call anybody a pig.

We moralize. We are horrified. Haven't we taught our children better than that? It's hard for us to take it on the ear. We forget that friendships are built by listening and finding out what's going on inside of our children.

Here's a way this mother could get in touch with Jed's feelings:

> Mother: You mean he *never* wants to share?
> Jed: Never! Nothing.
> Mother: It does seem selfish.
> Jed: Like a pig.
> Mother: Has Nathan *ever* shared *anything* with you?

9

Jed: I think half a Twinkie once.

Mother: Oh, maybe he's not a total pig, then.

Jed: Well, maybe not.

Mother: It sounds like you don't like stingy friends. I don't either. You'll probably want to be a friend who shares.

Jed: Yeah, I sure will.

Heather (age ten): Ow! Ow! I smashed my finger! It's terrible! I'll never be able to play the piano again!

Mother: It couldn't be all that bad—and besides, it's not going to get you out of practicing.

We don't understand the child's pain, we feel that a top priority is developing talents, and besides, we're paying through the nose for the lessons. Instead Mother might say:

> Ouch. I know that hurts. I'm so sorry. When you hit your finger that hard it hurts down to your toes. Come here and let me rub it and give you a squeeze. I love you, Heather.

Here are two examples of trying to talk teenagers out of their feelings:

Adam (age sixteen): I hate homework! Why do they always give it on the weekend?

Mother: It's not fun, but, if you don't study, you'll never make anything of yourself. The facts are that you've got to be vocationally as well as spiritually prepared these days.

We get uptight and try to persuade with logic. Isn't the glory of God intelligence? Aren't we raising not only missionaries but astronauts? True. Our logic is realistic and valuable, but our children need us to empathize with their feelings first. Later we can share our values and help them catch a vision of their future. Instead, Mother might say:

Mother: Weekend homework is a bummer! Don't they know that guys like to go skiing and to concerts on the weekend?

Adam: Yeah, are they crazy or something?

Mother: "All work and no play makes Jack a dull boy." Haven't teachers ever heard of that?

Adam: They don't have ears.

Mother: Nor hearts either, it sounds like.

Adam: Well, Mom, maybe they're not that bad. Part of the problem is that I should do a little more every day so I don't let my homework pile up on the weekend.

Mother: You're okay, Adam. You usually figure things out right.

Marie (age fourteen): I'm going to leave my room messy. I like it that way, so just be quiet about it.

Mother: Don't you talk to me that way, or you'll be grounded for a week. Now go to it, and start cleaning!

We threaten, order, and command. We can't have any semblance of filthiness in our homes and we're going to wipe it out in one fell swoop! Mother might have defused the tension by saying:

Mother: When I walked by your room, it looked as if there'd been an explosion, but I was glad to see that you hadn't been hit—or hurt.

Marie: Oh, Mom—it's not that I like to live in a cyclone, but my room is so little and I can't do it all—with homework and swim team. I've got too much going.

Mother: How can I help you?

Marie: Maybe you could get me some boxes so I could store things under my bed and help me decide what should go in them.

Mother: It's a deal! It's hard to keep things clean and organized in a tiny room with very little storage.

Since listening takes time, it's easy to place more importance on getting things done by *our* timetable than communicating caring to our children. At the moment, it seems easier to shape them up by moralizing, giving advice, persuading with logic, threatening, and commanding. These well-intentioned tactics, which we have all used at one time or another, block communication with our children and keep us from finding out their deeper feelings of anger, loneliness, frustration, or pain. Leading psychologists agree that these roadblocks to communication are the foundation of misunderstanding between parent and child.

On the other hand, if we listen long enough, with an open heart and mind, we will be able to relate to their feelings, which may seem exaggerated, but are real to them. Furthermore, we will not *feel* the same way about the problems between us, for now we understand them better.

Listen for Understanding

By allowing our children to fully share their feelings with us, we show our sincere regard for them. Fitzhugh Dodson, author of the best-seller *How to Parent* (Los Angeles: Nash, 1970, p. 322) says:

> The best way to keep your relationship with your child strong and meaningful is to show him that you genuinely understand how he feels about things. You can do this most convincingly not by glibly saying "I understand how you feel," but by putting his feelings into your own words and feeding them back to him. By doing this you will be actively trying to put yourself in his place and see the world through his eyes.

Claudia recalls: I used this skill with my fifteen-year-old and it helped me identify her fearful feelings.

Clarice: I'd like to try out for Belairs singing group at school, but I doubt that I'd get in.

Mom: You think Belairs are such a sharp group that you don't stand a chance?

Clarice: No, Mom. I have a good voice. It's just that loads of the really great singers at Bellevue High are trying out and I'm scared.

Mom: You feel that while you may be good, there are others trying out who could be better and that's frightening.

Clarice: Yeah, that's right. And besides, Mr. Taylor has never accepted a Freshman in the group and that's proof positive he won't consider me.

Mom: I see. The bottom line is you're afraid maybe you're too young for the group, no matter how good your voice is.

Clarice: Yeah, you got it Mom.

Mom: Well, honey, you've always been a little ahead of yourself. I'd like to encourage you to give it a try.

Clarice: OK, Mom, I think I will.

As I listened, Clarice began to clarify her own confusing feelings and to find solutions to her problem.

The steps to effective listening are:

- Listen carefully with an open heart.
- Picture in your own mind what the child is expressing.
- Feed back to her, in your own words, the feelings you have heard.

Dorothy shares: Having learned something about listening principles in a parenting class, I began using them, sometimes awkwardly. On one occasion, after feeding back to my fourteen-year-old her *exact* words (because I couldn't seem to think of any others), she became furious and yelled, "Don't do that to me!" She slammed the door and walked away. Later she again felt the need to express her feelings and called from the other room, "Okay, Mom, go ahead. Do me like you do me."

Even though I was frustrating her with my amateurish attempts, she was willing to put up with my efforts because she so much wanted to have her emotions heard.

After a few months of practice, I finally "got it." As I became increasingly able to sincerely respect my children, empathize with their feelings, and understand where they were coming from, the results were very exciting.

One Easter Sunday, my eight-year-old Stan came upstairs with his Easter basket filled with candy and eggs and announced that he'd had a "dumb day." I tried to get in touch with Stan's feelings. Since it was unclear to me what a "dumb Easter" meant to him, I said, "You seem disappointed."

"Yes, very," was his reply.

"I'm disappointed, too, because I wanted this to be an exciting day for you," I responded.

"Well, you were wrong. How could anybody get excited over a big hunk of chocolate?"

"You don't like chocolate?"

"No, I think it's yucky!"

"Stan, what would you have liked most of all to find in your Easter basket?" I questioned with a softened tone.

"Oh, a rabbit or a dog."

I took him in my arms and hugged him. "It must feel awful to want a rabbit or a dog so badly and wake up to only a chunk of dark chocolate."

"Yeah, you're right, but you say I can't have a dog because it will run on Zeke's grass, but Zeke's dog runs on our grass all the time!"

"You don't think that's fair, do you?" I questioned.

"It isn't fair, not one bit."

"I feel bad because I would like you to have not only a dog, but a dog pen to put him in." (I gave him the dog in fantasy) "Dogs are fun for boys. They follow a guy around and play ball with him."

"That's right, but you don't get it, Mom, because what I'd really like is a horse in the back yard. Then I could jump on him and gallop up and down the street and Zeke would say, 'Boy, I wish I had a horse instead of a dog!'"

"Oh, I'm getting it; it's not a rabbit or a dog, but a horse you want

. . . and you want it in the back yard."

"Yeah!"

"You want Zeke to know you have a horse. To you, that might even be better than a dog."

"You're right . . . Who owns that vacant property behind our back yard, anyway?"

"The governor is one of the people who oversees it. Why don't you write to him and see if you could keep a horse there?" I gave Stan the governor's name and the address of the state capitol. He spent the rest of the day hunting and pecking a letter on the typewriter to the governor.

Shortly thereafter, Stan received an answer! Throwing the letter down in disgust, he said, "Darn it, Mom, I can't have my horse in the empty field. The governor says there's a law that won't let horses live in the city limits. He's says he's sorry, but it's impossible."

I had listened without "erupting" on Stan. As a result, he was able to open his heart and share it with me. His disappointment had not revolved around a piece of sculptured chocolate after all, nor even around a dog. For him, they had been entwined with lots of hurt about not being able to have a beloved riding horse pastured in the vacant lot by our house so he could show off in front of Zeke. I was finally able to help Stan work through his feelings by allowing him to fully share his thoughts. If I had become disgusted and attacked him as an ungrateful child that Easter Sunday, I would have missed the opportunity to understand Stan's deeper feelings. I'm glad I listened heart to heart.

"I" Messages

If our children are encouraged to appropriately express their feelings, they begin to realize that it's okay for us to express ours also. We can honestly share our own positive and negative feelings with our children as long as we do not attack their personality or character. This is done by using first person statements such as:

"I feel angry . . . very, very angry when I see this room with pop-corn all over the carpet and nice clothes wadded up in a heap. I feel like screaming. I'm tired and I need help."

"When you swat your brother I get furious. Little brothers are not for hitting. Red lights go on all over in my mind when I see that behavior."

"I" messages preserve the dignity of our children while allowing us to openly and honestly express our feelings. Claudia says: Feeling distraught and at my wit's end, I used a series of "I" messages with my seventeen-year-old son, Elden. I had repeatedly asked him to check in with me when he got off work late at night. When he failed to do so, I became distressed and fatigued, waiting up for him night after night. Some nights I wouldn't hear him come in at all. I would wake up startled, run to his room, and be greatly relieved—but angry—to find him sound asleep. One morning at 3:00 A.M., I heard the door slam. Dragging my weary body to the entry hall, I shared my desperate feelings with him.

"Elden, I'm so glad to see you. I'm exhausted waiting up for you every night!"

"Well, why don't you go to bed? I didn't ask you to wait up."

"I *do* go to bed, but I can't seem to settle down and really rest."

"Why, Mom? Just go to sleep, and forget about me!"

"I'm not ever able to forget about you, honey. When it's late, I worry that you've had an accident or been mugged. I can't sleep with those thoughts running around in my mind."

"Mom, if any of those things happened, the police would call you."

"That may be true; but I need to hear your voice and know where you are to be able to really sleep peacefully."

"I'm sorry, Mom. I get busy with my friends and homework and I forget. I did call once and you were gone, but I left a message on your recorder."

"Yes. I remember that message. I appreciated it so much. Thanks, honey. I guess I just need more messages, more often."

"*You*" *Messages*

On the other hand, we unwittingly destroy the self-respect of our children by launching personal attacks. Often, such statements begin with "you," and they are dangerous because they undermine the dignity of our children. For example, the following "you" messages are threatening to a child's self-concept:

> "You are a dirty, sloppy kid to sit in a room like this watching T.V."

> "You are a naughty boy to hit your brother."

> "You don't deserve to go to the movie when you've been so inconsiderate."

"You" messages are like a sword striking at the vulnerable feelings of a child. They may pierce deeply enough to cause her to question her intrinsic worth and integrity.

When Things Go Wrong

Dr. Thomas Gordon reminds us that storms between parents and children can erupt in a regular and almost predictable sequence. The child does something wrong. The parent reacts with something insulting. The child reacts with something worse. The parent deals out some high-handed punishment, and the fight is on (*Teacher Effectiveness*, White Plains, NY: Longman, 1977).

Claudia adds: When Elden came in late, a "you" message sequence could very easily have led to this scenario:

> "I see you can't be trusted. You said you'd call, and you didn't."
> "People say I'm just like my mother."
> "You are so rude!"

"I know. It runs in the family."

"Go to your room!" (I would probably have been screaming or crying by this point.) "I don't want to hear another word out of you!"

And I probably *wouldn't* have gotten another word out of him because our friendship would have been damaged. Chances are, I wouldn't have gotten many phone calls either.

The fact of the matter is that Elden has not checked in a great deal although I have given him many, carefully constructed "I" messages. I have even written "I" messages in notes I've prayed over and put in his lunch sack. This technique is not magic and doesn't always solve the problem. It's no abracadabra. However, Elden and I are still friends, expressing our feelings honestly and appropriately. We still have a working relationship. Our mutual feelings of respect have not been destroyed.

Since every child is like a river, a composite of deep and shallow places, sensitive listening creates an environment in which the ebb and flow of emotions can be explored. Wading through the wide river of our child's feelings challenges the patience and creativity of us all.

Here are some life-lines you may want to try:

1. When time permits, lie on a blanket on the lawn and look at the stars. Use some of the following phrases to open conversation:
   What do you suppose. . .?
   How can you explain. . .?
   I'd be interested to know what you think about. . .
   I'd like to hear your opinion of. . .
   How do you see the future of. . .
   What's your favorite song?
   What do you look for in a movie hero or heroine?
   What are the biggest changes in school this year?
   Tell me about the neatest girls/boys in your class?
   Who is your best friend? Why?
   What's the most exciting thing that's happened this week?

2. Try to avoid moralizing, judging, or interrogating. One mother explains, "Once I get my child talking, I have to watch myself or the first thing you know, I'm moralizing or judging his opinions. I'm an expert at making a moral out of a mole hill or anything else. So, I consciously try to hear him out, and sometimes this takes an hour or more. If his opinions differ from mine I have learned not to gasp or get all excited but simply say, 'That's interesting. I hadn't realized you felt that way. I'm glad to know.' I have to admit that sometimes it's painful for me to know how he's feeling. But I'm willing to suffer so we can both learn. (There I go moralizing again!) If I can keep myself calm and hear him out, he changes my outlook, and I sometimes change my direction."

3. "When possible," suggests another mother, "set aside a few minutes when the children come home from school and just listen. I have a healthy snack ready, like apples and raisins or granola. Begin by asking 'How was your day?' They bubble over with enthusiasm when they know they have me captivated."

4. Walk or jog and talk with a child. Don't push for conversation, just let it happen. Begin with weather, scenery, the fresh air, and more meaningful communication will come. One mother says. "If I listen with sincere intent, my children will begin with superficial thoughts but soon will progress to their deeper concerns and problems. If my motive is to get some vital information out of them, I'm usually squelched. But if it's to listen for understanding, I'm usually gratified. I learn what's making them tick at the moment, and I don't see things in the same way again."

5. Try to let your children shine. When they are telling an experience, let them tell it as they see it. Try to not snatch a story, bicker about details, or interrupt. Treat their experience with as much regard as you would that of an intimate friend.

6. You may want to set aside some time after Sunday dinner to be available to any child who wants to talk. One mother reports, "Some Sundays nobody comes, but that's okay too. If my children are too busy for me, at least they know that I'm not too busy to schedule time for them."

7. When the occasion permits, take one child at a time on a church assignment. While driving to and from, there is time to visit about whatever is in the child's heart. A mother who does this reports: "For a time, my daughter Suzanne was concerned about her height. The boys often teased her at school. After venting her hurt and anger, we came up with several good responses like, 'Try it some time. The air is great up here!' She was able to laugh and I'm glad she didn't have to suffer alone."

8. Occasionally, use the telephone to keep in touch with children who live away. One mother writes that she calls her children when the rates are low and sets a timer to give herself limits.

9. You might try waiting up for dating teenagers. A midnight cup of hot chocolate and an hour of empathetic listening puts deposits in the emotional bank account. One mother says that she goes to bed with her husband, then gets up when the teenagers come home. "I'm too sleepy to moralize or preach—I just listen. I can find out more about their lives from 12:00 midnight to 1:00 A.M. than I could in a week by shooting questions."

10. Listen while you are doing chores together. The conversation doesn't need to be profound. Just enjoy talking with each other about trivia. Often, mothers help children discover how they feel about values when they are talking about the most common things. A mother wrote on her survey, "If my son and I can't talk about computers and airplanes, we probably can't talk about cocaine and AIDS."

11. If your family likes puzzles, put jigsaw puzzles together. A mother says, "Some of my best conversations evolve

naturally when the children and I are struggling over a long, complicated jigsaw puzzle. An uncompleted puzzle draws us together like a magnet. It takes several days to complete and somehow, we find ourselves ready to talk as we sift through those puzzle pieces."

12. You might try this formula: "Start talking only when you've listened at least as long as you plan to talk. It's old and trite, but that's why we have two ears and only one mouth."

13. React with a listening ear to children who are transmitting "I'm hurt" signals. For example, Rick had been irritable all evening. He teased his brothers, snapped at his mother, was moody, and didn't eat supper. His mother said, "Rick, you've been acting angry and upset tonight. Is it because of something I've said or done?" She put her arms around him and continued, "Is there anything you'd like to share with me?" Rick opened up and told his mother that he'd gotten his first "C" in algebra. He expressed fears that his mark would bring his final grade down. If that wasn't bad enough, he'd played a lousy game of basketball after school. But the very worst part of his day was a rejection note pinned to his locker from the girl he had wanted to take to the prom. "If I had reacted in anger to Rick's moody behavior," admits his mother, "I may have missed the opportunity to sensitively listen to his battered feelings and be his friend."

One of the finest gifts we can give our children is to listen to them and help them identify and express their feelings in an acceptable way.

Divided Laughter Multiplies Joy

"Laugh and joke with your children."
—President Ezra Taft Benson

$\mathcal{M}$ark Twain gave his mother an enviable epitaph when he wrote, "My mother had a great deal of trouble with me, but I think she enjoyed it."

Apparently, Mrs. Clemens knew how to laugh at life, honestly appreciating the humor in each day. We mothers can also learn to enjoy the humor in everyday moments and share it with our children. We are twice blessed when we are able to recognize the absurdity in our troubles and then laugh them off.

Filling our homes with the sunshine of laughter, we build valuable friendships with our children because laughter softens the tragedies and misfortunes in our lives and cements our relationships. Even though this matter of guiding our children to heaven is serious business, continually emphasizing the bottom line and missing the punch line may mean we sidestep a lot of joy.

Claudia remembers: Five-year-old Thomas had been quietly putting together puzzles in his room for half an hour. Finally, he called out to me in a pleading voice, "Mom, I want somebody to come in my room and enjoy me."

That is exactly the point! There are rewarding payoffs for us when we learn to laugh with our children and sincerely enjoy them.

Laugh with Your Children, Not at Them

If we laugh *at* our children, making them take the brunt of a joke, we can be thoughtlessly cruel. Children are much too vulnerable when their self-esteem is developing to absorb sarcasm without injury. Their sensitive feelings are damaged, and their minds can be filled with self-doubt and pain. And that's no joke.

Dorothy says: When we poke fun at our children, no matter how innocently, we harm our friendship with them. I unintentionally dealt a blow to my relationship with one of my daughters when I composed the words to our family Christmas card one year. Speaking to her about it recently, I was shocked to learn that she remembered every detail. She recalled, "I remember when I was in the sixth grade I wanted the part of the Christmas fairy in the Christmas play. Instead, I was cast as the stately Christmas tree! I was to be the tall background prop. Devastated, I came home sobbing."

"And what did I say?" I asked earnestly.

"You tried to comfort me and get me to laugh it off. But it was no laughing matter for me. In a few days, *you* began making up clever rhymes about each member of the family for our Christmas card, and presented them to us for our approval. When I read the part about me, I flushed and tears came streaming down my face."

"I wish I could remember what I wrote that wounded you so deeply. Maybe I could look back and find the card in our family history book."

"You don't need to," she replied, "I have the words memorized:
Kate is five foot eight and a beauty to see
She bumps into ceilings and sky hooks
And in the school play,
She'll be the Christmas tree.

"Everybody's neat accomplishments were in there, but not mine. I was just a gawky tree."

As we talked, tears spilled down her face and mine. It was unthinkable that I could have hurt so deeply a child whom I love so much. But I had.

Similarly, all of us may unknowingly deepen personal wounds in the lives of our children if we laugh at them or make them the object of a joke.

Laughter Teaches Children to Survive in the World

When we laugh *with* our children, we teach them how to step back and take a different perspective on things. A mother named Cherie stood on the front lawn of her neighbor's yard with her sixteen-year-old son, Kyle. He had just made the devastating discovery that the emergency brake of his old van had failed. It had rolled into the retaining wall of their neighbor's house and looked almost as crumpled as his face. He had worked hard and scrimped to buy it. Putting her arm around his shoulders, Cherie said, "It's okay, honey. At least you didn't get a parking ticket."

We may not always be able to laugh through our frustrating situations; but when we do, we take some of the discouragement out of them and also teach our children how to bounce back when the going gets rough.

> Youngsters who are given healthy doses of laughter—not ridicule, but gentle joy and loving smiles—learn how to survive in the world. They can laugh at the absurdities of a world which sometimes does its best to drive us mad. (Spencer Kinard, "The Gift of Laughter," *The Spoken Word*, March 1988)

Laughter Fosters Creativity

When our children see us laugh at our mistakes, we encourage creativity because they see that we have the courage to make clowns of ourselves. In the process, we teach them how to try new things and take risks. Trial and error are the basis of creativity.

C. W. Metcalf, founder and director of Body English, points out that a number of big corporations now tell their managers that if they don't make four or five mistakes a year, they may lose their jobs. Says Metcalf, "If you are not making mistakes, you're not trying new things and taking risks, and that's the only way you can be creative" ("Inspiring Innovations of Walt Disney World", *Park and Recreation*, Jan. 1985, p. 41).

Being able to genuinely laugh at our own mistakes shows our children that mistakes aren't fatal. Being able to laugh at their own mistakes helps our children risk sharing their ideas. It teaches them to have fun with a creative art form without being an expert in it. "All real works of art look as if they were done in joy" ("Motivation", an unpublished paper by Paul L. Harmon).

Indeed, laughter infuses our children with a sense that our faith in them and their ideas is greater than our fear. Such confidence is worth a million laughs.

Laughter Celebrates Life

When we laugh with our children, we teach them how to celebrate the joys of life. We teach them how to "lean into" the temporary and ordinary pleasures of each day as well as the extraordinary ones.

Scott Hamilton, who was a gold medal winner, once asked Eric Heiden, a five-times gold medal winner, how he withstood the pressure of competition. Heiden replied, "Enjoy it. You'll never have the opportunity again" (*Deseret News*, Jan. 18, 1987).

Each day holds its temporary nonsense, hilarity, and fun. If we seize these ridiculous moments with a laugh, we pass the tradition on to our children. Mark Twain said, "Grief can take care of itself, but to get the full value of joy you must have somebody to divide it with." Funny, but when we mothers divide a laugh with our children, the joy multiplies between us and it deepens our friendship.

Ideas That May Help You Avoid the Slivers as You Slide Down the Banister of Life

1. Collect your favorite joke books, cartoons, video cassettes, audio tapes, and funny gadgets. When you want to make a hit with the kids and relieve stress in a tense situation,

25

head for your "jest for fun" collection.

2. Try an eye-opening exercise. After a difficult experience involving anger, disappointment, and tears, attempt to stand back and see the scene as one you had to write for a TV sitcom. You may then be able to see the comedy in your situation and feel the magic release of the negative emotions. Humor can make disappointment less devastating, tension more tolerable, and bad days more bearable.

3. Write down on a note pad the funny things that have happened to you and your children. For example, the day you found the twins in the milk box, one cracking eggs over the head of the other one, or the time you used gold spray paint on some shoes for your daughter's prom date and most of the gold came home on her date's pant legs. Annette Goodheart, psychotherapist, points out:

    > We're happy because we laugh, not the other way around. The usual way of describing the process is that you have a sense of humor, so you laugh, and that changes your attitude. I start by laughing, which changes my attitude immediately. It's easy to fake laughter—your diaphragm doesn't distinguish between that and the real thing. It's like starting a car engine. The physical motion triggers real laughter. ("RX:Laughter", *McCall's,* Aug. 88, p. 106)

4. While you're doing a boring job like cleaning the kitchen cupboards, you could make up limericks. Kids love these nonsense poems which can be about members of the family, school teachers, friends, or imaginary people. A limerick has five lines. The first two and the last rhyme and the third and fourth rhyme. The third and fourth lines are shorter than the other three. Here's an example:

> There was a young brother named Sam
> Who loved peanut butter and jam.
> When he spread it on bread
> He nearly dropped dead
> From the weight in the palm of his hand.

5. Here's another giggly game that's especially good for younger children: "Little Sillies." This works great when you're in the car, swinging, or doing yard work together.
Mother: Two little sillies sitting on a seat
They got hungry and what did they eat?
First Child: French-fried trash.
Second child: Bubble gum sandwiches, and stir-fried shoelaces.
Third child: Hot fudge sauerkraut

6. Practice finding something to make you feel like smiling. A smile has an amazing power to send love messages to your children. One mother suggests: "Set a portable timer to go off at intervals. Carry it around with you; and when it rings, evaluate your expression. Determine if a smile from you can cause a mood miracle with those around you."

7. Have an "Oh Pun Season." Children can learn to make a "play on words" and become punsters, even punaholics. For example, Mother introduces the subject, "Birds."

"The game crows on you," says the first.
"Yes, but I'm feeling a bit hawkward," continues the second.
"Use your imagination and don't try to parrot what someone else has said," chimes in the third.

Practice at the dinner table, at the restaurant, or riding in the car. Punning makes for a very pleasant drive, until its time to start winging your way back home.

27

8. Jot down a good joke. Darleen, one of the mothers we surveyed, wrote: "I work at being playful. I understand that less than 2 percent of the population is capable of remembering and telling jokes. Since I am not one of those enviable few; when I hear a good one, I write it down for future reference. Then I'm able to tell it without forgetting the punch line! It may seem strange, but that's what I have to do. It's worth the time for me because telling a crazy story to my teenagers lets them know that their straitlaced mother can look at things in an offbeat way. It's a kind of relating that gives us a sense of joy in being together."

9. Collect your kids' cute sayings. Write them down immediately, for they can seldom be paraphrased and their logic cannot be recaptured. For example:

Six-year-old Thomas arose on a Sunday to find that the Tooth Fairy had not left anything under his pillow.
"Mom," he said, "the Tooth Fairy is late, but that's all right because she's a Mormon and doesn't work on Sunday."

Rachel: "There are so many things that cost money, like the fridge when we open the door. But 'cept, I don't know why 'cuz we already bought it."

Three-year-old Jacob couldn't get to sleep after stories, family prayer, private prayer, snuggles and numerous drinks of water.
Mother: "What *is* the matter, Jacob? Why can't you go to sleep?"
Jacob: "Mom, my eyes are too short."

Can you imagine the number of times Jacob's parents and grandparents have had eyes that were too short when insomnia struck?

Family jokes tie one generation to the next. They keep us laughing and loving. They add to the memory bank and the family humor storage. Even older children often come up with phrases worth jotting down.

The doorbell had rung three times and fifteen-year-old Clarice calls from the bathroom, "Mom, could you get that? I'm inexposed!" Clarice may have meant "indisposed", but her phrase has helped us all remember with a smile that the person most modestly dressed is elected to answer the door.

10. Compile a family book of sniglets. A sniglet is any word that doesn't appear in the dictionary but should. For example:

Seven-year-old Thomas was working with a clogged spray bottle. Making little headway in clearing the tubing, he exclaimed in a disgusted tone, "Just as I thought. It's *hydro cliometrated.*"

> *hydro cliometrated:* particles which occlude water flow.
> *skagle:* A crackly, hoarse quality in the voice.
> *combiloop:* Two or three unsuccessful tries at opening the combination locker.
> *flopcorn:* The unpopped kernels at the bottom of the cooker.

When you want to open a trap door under your stockpile of stress, read your family history of sniglets. If an out-of-this-world story using the name of a child will delight him, using his original words will put him into orbit.

The sunshine of laughter teaches our children to survive in a sometimes alien world, to stretch their minds with creative ideas, and to find joy in the present. And that's no laughing matter!

Music: Glad Notes in the Home

"Sing with them..."
—President Ezra Taft Benson

*C*laudia says: Seven-year-old Rachel and I had been working on a new piano duet, "That's an Irish Lullaby." An important errand prevented me from staying with Rachel during her next lesson where we were scheduled to play the duet for the teacher. When I picked her up after the lesson, I anxiously inquired, "Did you play the 'Irish Lullaby' for Mrs. Measle?"

"Yes," Rachel replied despondently, "but it sounded so lonely without you."

Music is a powerful form of communication when it is shared. Playing the duet *together* on the piano bench, Rachel and I participated in the joy of mutual expression. However, in my absence, much of the experience was lost for her.

Music has a poignant, unifying capacity when we learn to use it effectively to enhance friendships with our children. It may provide an outlet for unspoken feelings and help to build emotional bridges, even if we are not musically gifted ourselves. We *can learn* to use music to enlarge friendships with our children, and be a notable success at it!

Music strengthens mother-child friendships in three important ways:

1. It helps children express unspoken emotions and feelings, and this expressiveness carries over into relationships in a positive way.

30

2. It helps build emotional bridges.
3. It gives us a means for comforting our children.

How to Use Music to Help Children Express Feelings

Music can provide a wholesome outlet for the expression of children's feelings. President David O. McKay said, "There are feelings in the human breast which cannot be expressed in any language or words; so we must provide ourselves with other mediums of expression; for instance music" (*Pathways to Happiness*, Salt Lake City, UT: Bookcraft, p. 184).

Creative musical experiences provide an effective means for expressing feelings. They also allow children to relieve tension. We can encourage our children to express their emotions through music in any of the following ways:

1. Invite your children to "move" with you to music. Avoid using the word "dance" to discourage any stereotyped, stylized steps. Instead try using the following rhythmic descriptions.

Jumping:	long	big	slow
	high	fast	lazy
Walking:	big steps	on heels	knees out
	short steps	stiff legged	like ducks
	stamping	on tiptoe	goose step
	skating	like hens	sideways
	leaping	fast-slow	backwards

Swinging Arms: like a monkey, like a railroad signal, like tree branches, like windshield wipers, like an elephant's trunk, etc.

Bending and Stretching: stretch small-tall, stretch like a rubber band, stretch your face, stretch up to walk on stilts, stretch to see how tall-wide-small you can make yourself.

Pushing-Pulling: pull a wagon, row a boat, dig, swim, etc.

Twisting and Turning: Keeping feet stationary, twist your arms and torso around and around as you sink to the ground.

31

2. Suggest to your child that everyone has a musical instrument which he carries with him everywhere—his voice. A mother we surveyed wrote, "I tell my children that all of us are potential members of heavenly choirs someday, and that we need to keep in practice! It is a kind of disrespect to our Heavenly Father if we don't use the instrument he's given us." Elder Hugh W. Pinnock states, "Singing is an act of worship" ("Collection of Hymns, Old and New, Will Serve Varied Needs of Members", *Church News*, August 11, 1985).

3. Have fun as you put together a family rhythm band with your children. Rehearse on "bad weather" days. They may choose to assemble their own instruments. For example: Two chopsticks, empty metal pans with wooden spoons, pan lids for cymbals, sandpaper stapled around two blocks of scrap wood, rattles, microwave bacon rack with wooden spoons, rubber band around a shoe box, etc. Encourage everyone to play or dance until rosy cheeks reveal that energy has been released and emotions discharged.

4. Sing together. Let a song serve as a mood-setting invitation to home evening, scripture study, or family prayer. You may want to try playing a familiar song and leaving off the last few measures. It's a great way to get a response. Sing as you work, play, and travel together. In addition, sing hymns as lullabies, since a lullaby is synonymous with mother.

   "It has been my experience," says a mother of nine, "that the right kind of music can soften hearts and invite the Spirit of the Lord to be present when nothing else can. I often invite my children to sing with me. If there are angry feelings present, singing a tender song like 'I Know My Father Lives' often softens their hearts."

5. Prepare a family songbook using a loose-leaf binder and plastic covers. Have your children choose their favorite songs in various categories, for example: seasonal songs,

holiday selections, reverence and prayer songs, silly songs, etc. Use the book for long outings, vacations, and family activities.

Claudia reports: On the road to our family campout, Rachel, our seven-year-old, started on page 1 and sang to page 132 of our family songbook! Although other family members were chatting and laughing, Rachel sang for three hours. Intermittently, the other children joined her. It had been fun assembling our family song book, but it was even more fun hearing it.

6. Make a cassette tape with your children. Include favorite lullabies, camp songs, and inspirational melodies. Let the children help decide on the songs to be included in each category. Record their voices, letting each child take turns introducing the selection. Play and sing along with the tape at home, or in your car.

7. Use music to help eliminate contention. Tell the children they can express their disappointment or anger to brothers or sisters *if* they sing their feelings. Tamera, a mother who does this, says, "Contention gives way to loving humor because it is almost impossible to sing and remain angry."

How to Use Music to Build Emotional Bridges

Music has the capacity to build emotional bridges and happy memories with our children. Jack Christianson states, "Music is one of God's greatest tools for good ever created" ("Music: Apples or Onions?" *New Era*, April 1984).

Try these happy notes:

1. Try the game one mother told about in the *Ensign*: "We play *Name That Hymn*, adapted from the popular TV game show. I play one chord on the piano, and the children try to guess the title of the hymn. If they don't know it, I play two chords, and so on until they guess it. When we

33

first began playing the music game, we could identify about a dozen favorites. Now we know over one hundred beautiful hymns. We not only have the sounds of hymns ringing in our home, but we have their inspiring words written in our minds and in our hearts" (Adapted from "Name That Hymn," *Ensign*, April 1981).

2. Play "Clap That Song" with your children. "We clap out the beat of a well-known hymn or other favorite song to see who can guess it first," says Marcia, mother of a large family. "Listening carefully to the rhythm has acquainted us with several titles that fit the common rhythms. "We had a blast," laughs Mike, Marcia's teenage son, "going to ball practice or a music lesson trying to name the song while we were riding along. We really had to get our head in tick with Mom's rhythm."

3. Play a hymn or Primary song to set the mood for bedtime routines. One mother says, "My love of music came down through the genes. I believe mothers are the key to influence children in their attitude toward music. Sometimes instead of bedtime stories, my mother used to sing reverent or soothing lullabies in the evening. Then she'd play 'Softly Now the Light of Day' on the organ, which was a signal for us five daughters to march upstairs to bed. When we were bathed and clean, she'd come up and say prayers and tuck us in bed. Playing the hymn began a ritual as sweet as home itself, and one which I will never forget."

4. To create closeness between you and your children and to brighten somber moods, make up simple lyrics to familiar melodies. Personalize them with the names and activities of your younger children. For example: To the tune of "Catch the Sunshine," sing:

Catch your stocking, do it quickly,
quickly get your stocking on.

Or to the tune of "Onward Christian Soldiers":

Onward Jacob Middleton,

Marching as to war;
Let's pick all your toys up.
You will be a star.

When you're singing "He's Got the Whole World in His Hands," try lyrics like these:

He's got little, bitty Ellie in her brand-new dress
He's got Jan and Denny and their shining eyes
He's got the whole world in his hands.

Or to the tune of "Michael, Row the Boat Ashore."

Daddy helps us cook the soup
Hallelujah!
Amy helps to eat it up
Hallelujah!
Jason helps to wipe the spills
Hallelujah!

5. Borrow from the public library recordings of any music you like. One favorite is *Carnival of the Animals* by Camille Saint-Seans. Saint-Seans introduces children to the sounds of lions in a royal march, chickens, roosters, turtles, elephants, kangaroos, and swans. After hearing *Carnival of the Animals* as the concluding number at a concert, nine-year-old Rachel looked at her program and puzzled, "Mom, I can figure out kangaroos and turtles, but what are finales?" Sharing music with our children stimulates questions and helps us discover together.

6. Take your children to symphony rehearsals. Most are free of charge and provide a comfortable atmosphere in which children may whisper questions.

7. Listen *with* your children to a variety of musical forms, including jazz, opera, folk songs, western ballads, popular rock, musicals, symphonies, and spirituals. Claudia said: I scored a zero with my fifteen-year-old one evening when I belittled him with the question, "Do you think that tape you are playing is an appropriate choice of music?"

Defensive muscles tightened in his face as he replied,

"Mom, this is good music! Not all good music has to have violins in it!" That evening my son taught me that my definition of good music must not be so narrow that I silence our friendship.

8. Sing to your children. One woman recalls, "My mom had a lovely voice and once in a while she'd come in and sit on my bed and sing to me. I would usually request 'Way Down Upon the Swanee River.' I didn't like the song, but it was the longest one she knew and I wanted to keep her near me forever."

Give Comfort to Your Children

Music can be effectively used as a source of comfort. We can be "music therapists" to our children as we use music to improve morale and sociability during times of stress.

1. Sing around the home. Your voice, lifted in song, can be an important part of a pleasant home environment. Michael Moody, Chairman of the General Church Music Committee urges, "If you think you can't sing, sing anyway. So what if someone. . .says you can't sing. I say your best singing effort is beautiful" (*Church News*, Oct. 3, 1981, page 15). Dorothy recalls: On a recent visit to the home of my daughter, I sensed a great deal of tension surrounding their forthcoming move into a new home. Her twelve-year-old had been burdened by it for some weeks. I began baking while singing, "Let Me Call You Sweetheart." When I stopped momentarily to taste a cookie, my granddaughter, Tara, called out from the other room, "Sing some more, Grandma."

   "Oh, honey, I don't have a good singing voice," I objected.

   She replied, "Well, it's a good *hearing* one, and it doesn't matter one bit to me if it's not beautiful. It makes me feel better."

2. Play cassette tapes of Primary songs when your children

are sick or discouraged. Susan Christensen writes: "Our home caught fire last February and our nine-year-old daughter was badly burned. During her month in the hospital, she listened to her favorite music. The nurses wouldn't even begin her burn treatments without her Primary songs playing and they often commented on the beautiful songs. I was thankful she already had a love for good music, because it greatly helped us through that ordeal" ("How to Develop & Instill Love for Good Music", *Church News*, Mormon Forum, 28 Sept. 1986, p.15).

3. Branch out with cassette tapes of the hymns. They are now available either as instrumental accompaniments or with voices added to the instruments. Elder Hugh W. Pinnock states, "Hymns can provide strength and support in much the same way as the scriptures" (*Church News*, 11 Aug., 1985).

4. Sing or whistle while you work. Elicia and Tara got up at 3 a.m. to weed the garden and surprise their tired parents. As they quietly worked by the light of the moon, the howling of neighborhood dogs and other strange noises filled them with terror. To drive away their fear of the dark and lighten their task, they sang favorite family songs. Often they clutched each other tightly and sang softly. Other times they giggled quietly as they sang funny family favorites.

5. Sing hymns and other sacred songs with your children. Sacred music has the ability to soothe and comfort despondent souls. It can facilitate feeling the Spirit and bring solace to heavy hearts. Dorothy recalls: I shall never forget the day my brother, Paul, was hit in the right eye with a piece of flying metal while he was working in his high school shop class. An emergency trip to the doctor revealed that my seventeen-year-old brother would be blind in one eye for the rest of his life. I remember the feeling of gloom that penetrated our hearts as we surrounded the daybed where Paul rested with a patch over his injured eye. As

the shadows lengthened into evening, we all found words a burden. We were silent and heart-weary. Finally, my sister, Geraldine, went to the piano and began to play:

"I know that my redeemer lives."

Dad joined her singing:

"What comfort this sweet sentence gives."

Although we were choked up and crying, Mother and I joined in singing:

"He lives to comfort me when faint. He lives to hear my soul's complaint."

We sang all four verses together, and the music seemed to lift us up to touch heaven.

Music reaches the hearts of children at any age. Let's add some glad notes to our relationships and sweeten the score.

How to Catch Minutes to Make Memories

"Spend unrushed one-to-one time with each child."
—President Ezra Taft Benson

Lorraine once asked her fifteen-year-old son, John, what experience he remembered best from his early childhood. Without hesitation, he said, "The night on the way home from my Cub Scout outing, when you stopped the car on a dark road and helped me catch fireflies."

Lorraine barely recalled the incident, but John remembered. He knew his mother was in a hurry to get back home to her own work, and he thought she wouldn't stop. But she did! Lorraine said, "What I *did* that night said 'I love you' more than any words could have said. I often wish now that I had kept my priorities in perspective and taken advantage of more spontaneous activities like that with my son."

John felt his mother's friendship the night they caught fireflies. It was so important to him that he tagged it as his "best" childhood memory. But if Lorraine had grumblingly stopped the car and begrudgingly caught fireflies, John wouldn't have *felt* the same thing!

Psychiatrist Dr. Ross Campbell states: "Focused attention is the most demanding need a child has. . . It is not something that is nice to give our child if time permits, it is a critical need" (*How to Really Love Your Child*, Wheaton IL: Victor Books, 1977, p. 68).

Love is an action verb which says to our children "I'm enjoying our time together. You are worthy of my time. Your interests are important to me. In fact, at this moment you are the most important person in my life. You light up my life like fireflies."

Making lasting friendships with our children is based on spending time with them. That's how our children make memories that can be stored and recaptured when they need to remember that they are loved. Such positive memories forge meaningful ties.

Solving the Problem of "Taking Time"

One seminary teacher reports that he assigns his students a seven-minute mother-student communication quiz which must be done using eye-to-eye contact. It often takes over two weeks for his students to finish the assignment!

In contrast, a busy mother of four boys, sets aside every Wednesday afternoon to spend with one of her four sons. She declines all meetings and luncheons, no matter how elaborate or exclusive, if they are held on Wednesday.

Another mother began making a date with each of her children and writing it in her planner. She made this decision after her eight-year-old, Jason, announced, "I know why you don't have time to play with me, Mom. In your little, black planner book, I can't find my name."

Capture Spontaneous Moments

Sometimes building happy memories means capturing spontaneous, unscheduled moments with our children and capitalizing on them.

Barbara writes, "I've heard mothers say that it doesn't matter how *much* time they spend with their children, but rather that it's the *quality* of time that counts. I agree that quality time is important; however, I never know when a block of time will open up in the lives of my children. When it does, I want to be available and willing to fill it up with spontaneous fun."

Barbara is right. Neither she, nor any one of us, can schedule fireflies. Experiences with our children probably won't be memorable if we, in a panic, insist, "I've got twenty minutes, so let's make it quality."

What is vitally important to us (and our time frame) may have little importance to our children. We create a backdrop for happy memories when we are willing to respond spontaneously. Claudia says: One afternoon when my twins turned nine, I was in the midst of preparing for separate parties on the same day. As I was decorating the two layer cakes, my seventeen-year-old, Elden, and his buddies arrived on the scene. They hungrily sniffed hot dogs and chips as Elden announced, "Hey, all right! We've happened on a party. How about that?" The boys were headed for a movie, but Elden thought they could squeeze in a party. I had mixed feelings. On one hand, I was relieved to even *see* Elden. He had been too busy to use home for much more than a pit-stop. Sometimes I wondered if I really knew how tall he was because I only saw him stretched out horizontally between the sheets. Now was my chance. On the other hand, I still had balloons to blow up and party favors to assemble.

Looking again at Elden's curly hair and steady smile, I decided to have another party. I began to set the table with red, plastic plates. Happily, Elden joined me to add the relish and the sparkling grape juice. The teens ate hungrily, laughing as Elden presented the twins with a dinosaur punch-out book he'd picked up for their birthday. Within minutes, my unexpected guests filled their stomachs and rushed out the door. Although I invited them to come back later for cake and ice cream, they never did. As I washed the red plastic plates for the next party, I pondered the experience. Time with Elden was as difficult to capture as dandelion dust and maybe my best times with him would come spontaneously and inconveniently, like today, when he just "happened on a party."

Be Willing to Bend

Dorothy says: We had made plans to go boating with our five children on Lake Powell. We would be very crowded during the seven-hour ride to the lake in our jeep, but wasn't that what families were for—being together? Sixteen-year-old Stan had different ideas. He announced that instead of making the trip with the family, he'd like to bicycle the 350 miles with his buddy, and meet us there.

Although he was an experienced cyclist, his ideas frightened me. All I could think of was the lengthy distance, the scarcity of water, and the blistering desert sun. Surely bicycling would be dangerous. I felt desperate, but Stan was determined, and I could see that it could be damaging to the relationship if I didn't help him, instead of fight him. When children are little, we don't go along with plans we feel might be dangerous; but when they are older, we must often balance the danger of the activity against the danger to the relationship. I began working with Stan on his plans.

Together, we looked at maps of Utah and Arizona. Stan calculated distances, plotted bicycle routes and motel locations. We noted specific sunrise and sunset times as Stan planned his cycling during the cooler hours of each day.

My part in the project was to bury bottled water at critical points in the desert along the way. I added snacks and poetic notes of encouragement. I also planned to be part of a cheering section to welcome the boys over the finish line.

A few hours before Stan's estimated arrival, the Lake Patrol notified us of the accident. I had a sinking feeling as I listened to the details. Stan's bicycle tire had caught between the metal ribs of a cattle guard. The bicycle had remained stationary while Stan was thrown into the air, landing heavily on the shoulder of the highway.

Minutes later, I felt a rush of panic as Stan emerged from a patrol car and I saw his bleeding face. We should have stuck to our original plans and none of this would have happened, I thought. Why hadn't I been stronger when I talked about the dangers of cycling such a distance?

When Stan felt like talking, he re-lived the specifics of the last 300 miles. He had found the buried water. The pyramid stone markers had worked. The water had been buried at the proper intervals. His calculations had been right. The motel stops had coincided with his need for rest at the right time. He had enough energy treats and snacks to keep him going. In fact, everything had gone *just* as planned. The only hitch was that he had gotten up a half hour too early on the last leg of the journey and there had not been quite enough light to see the cattle guard. He *seemed* to regret that error in his planning more than his injuries. Overall, he felt good about his plan. The fact that it didn't work perfectly wasn't so important to him as that most of it *had* worked. In fact, he began almost immediately to plan a cycle trip for the next year. "And Mom," he said through swollen lips, "you don't have to bury a Shakespearian sonnet with *every* bottle of water."

Although our children's plans may not always work out perfectly, we strengthen our relationship with them when we genuinely try to spend time in the way that means the most to them. Sometimes their terms may seem unreasonable and even dangerous, and young children may need to be guided to safer alternatives. However, when we make an effort to see activities from *their* perspective and join them in *their* plans, we bond ourselves to them. Then, if things don't work out exactly right, we have still shared a meaningful experience together and deepened our friendship.

Combine Everyday Experiences with Positive Feelings

We Americans annually spend a whopping $244 billion on recreation and recreational products. This amounts to one dollar out of every nine spent by a typical household (*American Legion Magazine*, June 1987, p. 22). However, even with this astronomical amount spent in recreation, family togetherness does not always occur. We can be emotionally apart even when we are physically together unless there is shared warmth.

Building friendships with our children means lacing everyday experiences with positive feelings. Often, happy memories grow out of very common, real-life activities. These memories fill the corners of our children's minds with sights, sounds, and smells that fill their hearts as well. They might include the happy feeling surrounding picking blackberries, buying pectin, and making jam together in the kitchen. They could include helping to make five Halloween Alley Cat costumes, spraying Eric's old car electric blue and purple, and growing crystals for the science fair. They may also include jogging, rowing, bicycling, and dieting together, or doing anything that is pleasant for you.

Dorothy says: I remember building a memory while doing dishes. Clearing the patio table one summer evening, my six-year-old, Kristen, made numerous trips to the back yard. She was attracted to the array of large stars she noticed in the sky that night. Finally, picking up some silverware she queried,

"Where do the stars come from?"

"Heavenly Father made them."

"How did he do that?"

"He took the elements that existed."

"Did he make the moon and the sun, too?"

"Yes, he put them in place and made the moon to shine at night and the sun to warm us by day."

"Then did the animals come?"

"Yes, Heavenly Father made the horse, like the one in our corral, and the cows, and the sheep. . ."

"How neat!"

"Then he made men and women and beautiful little girls like you to enjoy his lovely earth."

"Then what did he do?"

"He rested because he was all finished."

"Well, the sweet ol' thing!" exclaimed Kristen. "What's he doing now?"

"I think he's smiling because we're here *together* talking about him."

Meaningful togetherness means sharing positive feelings. It is giving our time, more than our toys.

Happy memories are made with our children when we spend both scheduled and spontaneous blocks of time with them. Friendships

44

are deepened when we participate in activities our *children* define as important. Even simple experiences become meaningful when we share warm feelings. These kinds of memories make the common routines of life uncommonly sweet.

Friendship Makers That Won't Break the Bank

A memory file could be created on 3x5 cards, including activities and ideas like these:

1. Ask each one of your children: "What are your best memories? Your worst?" Plan future activities around the responses you get.

2. Make an A-Z list of spots in your city which you and your child would enjoy visiting. Pull out the list when you could go somewhere. Don't try to squeeze in too much. Take time to sit in the shade and drink lemonade or have ice cream or hot chocolate. Listen. Get in touch with feelings.

3. Exchange houses or apartments with another family you know well. Take fastidious care of property as you spend a day or a weekend in a new and different environment, spending special time with each child.

4. Invite a child's friend to dinner. Make it a very merry un-birthday surprise.

5. Make bread together. Teenagers like to make twisted bread and cinnamon rolls. Younger ones like to make the dough into shapes of animals, even roll out an entire zoo and eat it with butter and jam.

6. Have crazy days. If it's raining, pack a picnic and eat under a canopy at the park. Have the lights out when the children come to dinner. Tell them you are preparing for a power outage. Eat by candle light. Freeze snowballs, fill the ice chest with them and go into the canyon for a snowball fight in July.

7. Go "sniping"—looking for make-believe creatures in the

woods. These little fellows may be hiding behind tree trunks, on branches, or under fallen logs or rocks. If you pretend to catch a big one, you may want to let him go; if he's little, pretend to feed him, pet him, or hug him. Let your imagination go. Make-believe that you're wrestling with a monster, outwitting an owl, or tangling with a bat. Pretend that you fly away with a creature half human, half bird. Try to convince your fellow snipers you have captured the most fantastic critter in the woods.

8. Help your child develop friendships with others. Together prepare a basket of homemade goodies or create a silly poem about friendship. Go along to deliver them to a child's friend.

9. Try making a cloth-bound book of blank pages with a child. Let the child choose a favorite picture of himself and paste it in the book. Together as the year rolls by, decide with the child what drawings, letters, and stories to paste in the book which tells best about him and his ideas. Enclose the sheets in plastic so that even small children can delightfully explore their chronicles without marring the pages.

10. Go bird watching, insect hunting, cloud musing, or star gazing. Try to pick out shapes of animals, vegetables, cartoon characters, friends, or relatives as you chuckle together about the funny ones.

11. Dress a doll in the outfit in which your child was blessed. Put her hospital I.D. bracelet around the doll's arm and hang her newborn picture around its neck.

12. Choose a VIP or child of the week. Invite him to sit next to you at the table, ride next to you in the car, shop with you at the grocery store, run errands with you on your day off, help you pay the bills, open your mail, or put down the tips when eating out.

13. Have wiggle and giggle time. Put on a funny tape or record and laugh together as you roll on the floor, tumble, toss, bounce, wiggle waggle, rock, reel, swing, and sway. It's

a law of nature that energy must be released. Burn it up, shake it out, and toss it over in your own family room or back yard.

14. Have a tea party any time your child and a friend come in together after school. With the varieties of herbal tea available, there can be that many different spicy occasions.

15. String a cord from the doorknob to a chair, throw a sheet over it, and stake out the ends with a few books. Crawl into the tent and read mystery stories or tell ghost stories to your children by flashlight.

16. Help a child with his homework.

Sixteen-year-old Daniel, an honor student, washed and vacuumed the family van just before his cousin came to borrow it for his family's vacation. That night at 11 o'clock after searching in every possible spot, he remembered that his history book with his class notes was in the van, fifty miles away, and he had a history test in the morning. He approached Tamera, his mother, who was tired from a full day of teaching, and asked for help. Her first thought was to borrow a book, but they couldn't borrow personal notes and the class outline. Responding to Daniel's desperate feelings, she drove the hundred miles while he got his other assignments done and arrived home to a grateful son and an armful of hugs. They both got up at 5 a.m. so Tamera could tutor Daniel for the test.

Tamera says, "First we knelt in prayer and I thanked the Lord for my fine son, his integrity, industry, and consideration for our family. When I finished the prayer, Daniel was sniffling and said he thought he might have a cold coming on. Then, in that early dawn, we thought of ways to memorize dates and places, and even shed a few tears over Washington at Valley Forge and what the flag meant to us. But most of all, we reinforced what we meant to each other."

Mothers are important catalysts in creating happy moments. We can make a few precious memories in a precious few minutes. Hopefully some of them will flicker brightly and light up the lives of our children like fireflies.

Give Them Warm Fuzzies—
Their Style

"Hug them."

—President Ezra Taft Benson

*E*xpressed affection is a life-sustaining power that helps build warm friendships with our children. There is a healing quality to touch which is closely aligned to the procreative power itself. When we pick up a crying newborn, let a cranky five-year-old climb into our lap, hug a ten-year-old, or put an assuring arm around a teenager, we are giving more than comfort. We are providing a warmth as necessary to a child's development as food and air.

"It is a mother's caress that first awakens a sense of security; her kiss the first assurance that there is love in the world " wrote President David O. McKay (*Gospel Ideals* p. 452, 1953).

At any age, our children require the warmth and security provided by our caring touch. Clare, a single mother of five children, recounts the difficulties she experienced with Greg, a teenage son, who became increasingly withdrawn and noncommunicative when his father left the home to marry another woman. She consulted a psychologist for help and was advised to give him back rubs after football games and practices. Gradually, her gentle, caring hands encouraged him to relax, open up, and disclose some of the aches in his heart. Subsequently, he was able to face the realities of his situation with greater confidence and to express gratitude to his mother for her healing touch.

When a Child Pulls Away

We can also show sincere affection for a child by being sensitive to cues that he is uncomfortable with physical closeness. If a child steps back or pulls away when we approach him, he may need space to work out his own feelings before he can include us in them. We can innocently distance him from us if we try to force physical closeness when he is not ready to receive it.

Louise recalls her feelings of utter rejection when her daughter, Sharilyn, began to pull away from her show of affection. "As a child, Sharilyn liked to be kissed, hugged, and caressed, but as she reached her teens, there was a gradual change. She stepped away if I even touched her to straighten a strap, arrange a belt, or fix a lock of hair. She'd turn up her nose, hump her shoulders, and snap, 'Don't touch me!' Sometimes she'd shudder and groan, 'I can't *stand* it when you hug me.'

"I have a naturally warm personality, and it's easy for me to show affection by touching, hugging, or patting. When Sharilyn stepped away from me, my feelings of rejection were very real. I had to learn that there could be emotional closeness between us even when there was little physical closeness. I felt less rejection when I came to *understand* that it is normal for teens to pull away because intimacy takes on a different meaning for them as they mature. I found I actually promoted emotional closeness between us when I respected her need for distance."

Non-touching Hugs

If you have a child who shies away from your embrace, you might want to try some of the following:

1. Rock a child in a hammock or push a pre-schooler in a swing, even though he is able to pump himself as high as he wants.
2. Give a child a stuffed rabbit with a love message such as: "Some bunny loves you."

3. Put a sign on a cookie jar, "Here's a big hug for you."
4. Use love stickers with hug themes. Many are found in stationary stores.
5. Write a note on a pad which has been printed "Hugs from the desk of Mom."
6. Throw a kiss to your child; smile lovingly.
7. Wink at him and tell him you have just given him a hug.
8. Sing a wacky song with made-up words about a child's attributes and set them to a familiar tune. For example: This one is set to the tune of "Oh Danny Boy."

> Oh Danny Boy, the pizza, pizza's calling.
> It's ready now, as ready as can be.
> Come handsome one, enjoy the pepperoni,
> For it will show, will show my love for thee.

Or here's one for a toddler:

> He's Daddy's little man, Daddy's frying pan,
> Mamma's little angel, Mamma's little boy,
> Daddy's little honey, Mamma's pride and joy.

Laura reports that this song became a "round" in her home because it went "around and around" until either she or her baby fell asleep.
9. Write "I love you" on the bathroom mirror with lipstick, shaving cream, or mascara.
10. Have a T-shirt printed with a personal message like "Thomas the Terrific," "The Remarkable Reading Rachel," "Electrifying Elden," or "Clarice the Clever."
11. Write "I missed you" on the sidewalk with chalk when a child returns from a short vacation.
12. Hang a balloon in a child's bedroom with a message in marker pen like, "You give me a lift" or "Sooner or later, great people like you rise to the top."
13. Write "You make life a ball around here" on a colorful ball and toss it to a child.

14. Make a heart-shaped puzzle for a child with personal thoughts about her, or glue a love poem or silly verse on the heart. Cut it into puzzle pieces and put it in her lunch sack, pants pocket, or suitcase.

15. Play an "I love you how much" game with a young child. Say, "I love you more than all the leaves on the trees." Ask him to respond with any silly comparison like, "I love you more than all the flies in the skies, sand on the shore, bees in the hive, bats in the belfry," etc.

16. Write a love note to a child. Roll it up tightly and slip it inside a colorful balloon. Blow up the balloon and write the message on it, "I love you so much, I'm ready to pop." Suggest the child pop the balloon to read your secret message.

17. President Spencer W. Kimball suggested baking a pie with a heart carved in the crust.

18. Mail a child a love letter, even when you haven't left town. Mention specific behaviors you have appreciated about him.

19. Cut out a red heart from construction paper. Attach a colorful string to the heart and write on it, "Here's my heart." Tuck it in a child's school book, sock drawer, backpack, purse, etc.

20. Make up bedtime stories in which your child is the hero or heroine. Base the stories on real life situations in which your child has overcome fears or performed well in difficult situations. For example: "Once upon a time there was a little boy named Thomas who wanted very much to make a project for the science fair at his school, but he didn't have any money to buy the magnets he needed for his idea. Finally, Thomas figured out a way to make money by delivering newspapers in his neighborhood once a week. Soon, he saved enough money to buy six magnets to build a generator for the science fair."

In essence, these kinds of "non-touching" hugs provide comfort and reassurance to our children at any age, without encroaching on their private space. When Louise refused to physically intrude into Sharilyn's emotional space without her permission, she showed genuine respect for her and created a climate of trust. This trust usually frees a child to confide in her mother about her hurts any time she feels emotionally able to do it.

Touching Hugs

When our children show that they enjoy a warm touch and we respond by giving one, we create a connection which carries positive, loving implications. Rita recalls, "As a teenager, I seldom came into the house after school without my mother pulling me to her. Often she sat me on her lap and rocked me like a baby. I loved to put my head on her chest and hear the rumble of her laugh. We both thought it was funny—me, a teenager—but I loved it!"

Some psychologists feel that caring can, in fact, be measured by the amount of time and energy mothers dedicate to physical availability. The soft touch soothes pain, decreases hurts, softens life's blows, and makes a child feel safe and loved.

Hugs say, "Your loss is my loss," at a time of deep disappointment; "I'd like to be your friend," when a child is feeling alone or forsaken; "I'm here and I care," when a child is feeling hurt; "You belong," when a child is feeling left out; or "You can feel secure here with me," when a child needs the feeling of protection and safety. In addition, a hug says:

"Come into my arms and stay here until you feel strong enough to go it alone."

"I'll help you."

"I trust you. I value you."

"You are wonderful and worthy of my time."

"I appreciate you."

"I'm happy to be with you. Let's celebrate!"

If our children are willing, we can reach out to them in some of the following ways:

1. Give a good rejuvenating hand, foot, or back massage. This demonstrates that we understand a child's fatigue, and want to decrease his hurt.

2. Give a "bear" or "ladder" hug. A bear hug is a full body hug. In a ladder hug, you hug only at the shoulders like a step ladder that hinges at the top.

3. Hold a child who needs comfort. Four-year-old Katie Marie, was burning up with fever. "Hold me, Mamma, hold me," she pleaded. Mother responded willingly with 7-Up, a cold cloth, and cuddles. After a time, she laid Katie in her bed again. Still, Katie looked up coaxingly, "Hold me longer, Mamma, longer." Mother picked up Katie again. Katie had expressed her need and Mother responded.

4. Plant a kiss on the palm of a child's hand. Fold his fingers tightly around it and ask him to hold it safely for a later time when he needs to remember that you love him.

5. Draw the letters in "I love you" on a child's arm, back or hand. Ask her to spell the message out loud.

6. Ask a child to "give me five," clapping your hands together with his in five different ways while repeating, "I love you so much."

7. Pretend you are making a loaf of bread with your child. The special ingredient will be "love" and you are going to "knead" this love throughout the loaf. Pretend the child's tummy is the dough while you "knead" and gently "punch down" the rising dough. Tell her your love makes the bread rise. Spice the loaf with tickles and hugs.

8. Make a copy of the following poem. Pin it near the rocking chair to remind you to take time to comfort a child and hold him close whenever he needs it:

Cleaning and scrubbing can wait 'til tomorrow
For babies grow up, we've learned to our sorrow
So quiet down, cobwebs, dust go to sleep
I'm rocking my baby, and babies don't keep.
(Nick Stinnett and John DeFrain)

Appropriate expressions of affection help build lasting friendships with our children because loving touch has a life-sustaining, healing power. It blesses and consoles like the healing power of the priesthood.

Before his ascension, the Savior visited the Nephites. He established his church among them and let them feast on an outpouring of his love in a wonderful way. It is significant that his *final* gesture was to touch "with his hand the disciples whom he had chosen, one by one, even until he had touched them all, and spake unto them as he touched them" (3 Nephi 18:36). Immediately afterwards, a cloud overshadowed the multitude, and he ascended into heaven.

Similarly, we mothers have the power to give our children confidence, comfort, and security as we touch their hearts and hands with genuine love.

Praise with Purpose

"Honestly praise your children."
—President Ezra Taft Benson

One of the most important skills in building friendship with our children is learning how to give sincere praise. Effective praise requires us to remember a few, simple ideas.

Like a mirror, we can reflect back to our children the unique qualities we discover in them. Cockney flower girl Eliza Doolittle, the leading character in the charming musical, *My Fair Lady*, based on George Bernard Shaw's play, *Pygmalion*, explained, "The difference between a lady and a flower girl is not how she *behaves* but how she is *treated*."

We may not always give our verbal approval in the most effective way; but each time we succeed, we build the self-esteem of our children and improve our friendship with them. Ultimately, they will come to understand that we love them for what they are as human beings *before* we love them for what they can do.

Effective praise, then, means that we learn how to make a distinction between our children's present behavior and what we believe to be their future potential.

Each child needs to be genuinely valued simply because he is himself. There is none other exactly like him, and we mothers are in a privileged position to tell our children this truth. Although they do not always perform perfectly or even admirably, we must not confuse temporary mediocrity of performance with mediocrity of the soul. The truth we need to recognize and help our children feel is that they are valuable because they are an incomparable creation of God.

Acceptance Can Be Felt

Dorothy says: Unconditional regard can be *felt* by our children. When six-year-old Kristen came home from visiting my friend, Myrl Hamilton, I was concerned. I knew she had gone over to visit Myrl twice that week already. I threw up my hands and cried, "Not again! I'm afraid if you go to Sister Hamilton's one more time this week, she'll get tired of you."

"Not Sister Hamilton," she assured me. "She likes me."

"How do you know?" I questioned.

"Because people knows when people likes people."

My little Kristen was right. Acceptance is warm and *felt*. It overlooks imperfection and motivates positive behavior. It nurtures the developing self-esteem of our children. In fact, acceptance feels so good, it's worth visiting Sister Hamilton three times in one week just to bask in it!

The Need for Verbal Reassurance

Dorothy says: Even as a small child, Stan regularly picked up his toys and lined up his toy boxes in our playroom. I was grateful for his tidiness. As a teenager, when I asked him to clean the car, he also took out the floor mats and trash containers and scrubbed them. In fact, he took out everything but the windows and engine, so he could detail it like those on a used car lot. I appreciated his obvious efforts.

When he studied trumpet, he arranged his own recital, sending out hand-written invitations. I was impressed with his self-reliance and organization. As an honor student in high school, he wrote and typed his own term papers, even ironing the pages that got wrinkled as he shuffled them around his desk. He earned his Eagle Scout and Duty to God award with the same persistence he displayed when he hobbled through the snow with his leg in a cast to play the piano for priesthood meeting. To me, his overall performance seemed exceptional.

One afternoon Stan began talking to me about applying for early college admission. I immediately told him to "go for it." I knew he could do it. I was surprised at his response.

"Mom, I don't know if I even *want* to go for it. I try and try. I nearly bust a gut—and yet I never seem to do anything good enough—at least, not good enough to get a pat on the back. When I get to the Pearly Gates, I expect St. Peter to say, 'I've been expecting you, Stan, but what in the world has taken you so long?'"

Why had I neglected to tell him how much I appreciated his achievements? I had certainly told him in no uncertain terms how disappointed I was when he brought home twenty gas caps from neighborhood cars or when he sank the motor of his red canoe in Lake Powell.

Our children need a lot of verbal pats all along the way. They need them long before they reach the pearly gates. In fact, without them, they may not feel their worth enough to keep striving toward heaven. It may seem like heaven is too far away to matter much right now.

Honest Praise at Any Age

People at any age need acceptance and honest praise, no matter how long or how public their list of achievements becomes. They still want their efforts to be noticed and appreciated.

On one occasion, President Joseph Fielding Smith and Sister Jessie Evans Smith were guests at a university fireside. President Smith gave a scholarly sermon and Sister Smith sang a solo in her rich, contralto voice. Then, sitting together on the piano bench, the Prophet and his wife sang a touching duet. The students were so inspired that they spontaneously arose after the closing prayer and sang "We Thank Thee O God for a Prophet."

The sister who had been in charge was deeply stirred and decided to write a thank-you note immediately upon her return home. As she was doing so, the telephone rang.

"This is Sister Jessie Evans Smith calling. Please tell me," she said a bit shyly, "how did we sound this evening?"

The sister assured her that the song was unforgettable. "I can still hear the melody in my mind," she said. "It had such an imploring quality to it."

Then Sister Smith asked, "How did we look on the piano bench together? I was afraid if I sat in front of the President, I'd cover him up, and I'd never want to overshadow the Prophet."

"It was one of the most appealing and tender moments of the evening," replied the sister.

"Oh, thank you," said Sister Smith. "We were a little nervous performing for the university students."

"Seeing you together made us all feel such warmth in our hearts," returned the grateful sister.

"Oh, that's good," Sister Smith continued with a relieved sigh. "We were getting ready to go to bed and we knew that we could sleep better if we just heard someone say that we'd done okay."

If Sister Smith, in her capacity as a first lady of the Church, needed reassurance that she had performed well, it is not surprising that *all* of Heavenly Father's children require similar approval.

Praise Is Emotional Medicine

Praise is like penicillin. In order to be effective, it has to be administered cautiously. The most meaningful praise includes four important elements:

1. It describes how the child's behavior affect you.
2. It is honest and realistic.
3. It deals with the child's efforts and accomplishments, rather than his or her character.
4. It avoids any attempt to manipulate behavior.

Describe How the Behavior Affects You

When we specifically describe how a child's behavior affects us, the child draws his own conclusions about himself. For example:

Mother: Your talk gave me some new ideas about baptism.
Child (infers): I *did* have some good thoughts. I must be pretty smart to have come up with them.

Mother: Your collage makes me feel quiet and peaceful.
Child (infers): I am good at putting things together. I'm creative.

Mother: Your story spoke to my heart.
Child (infers): I can write good stories.

Mother: Thanks for returning the money when I overpaid you. I appreciate it.
Child (infers): I'm a person who can be trusted. It feels good to be honest.

When we honestly tell our children how their behavior makes us feel, our words are like a canvas upon which they can paint their own picture of themselves.

Be Honest; Don't Exaggerate

Dr. Haim Ginott claims that exaggerated praise is as uncomfortable for our children as direct sunlight. It may even blind them so they can't see their real strengths, and it puts them in a position of having to shield themselves from unrealistic statements. They may even deny part of a sincere compliment (*Between Parent and Child*, McMillan Co, NY, p 38-40). For example:

Mother: You are a genius on the piano.
Child (infers): How could I be? I haven't finished playing the pieces in Book 3 yet.

Mother: You are the best worker in the entire world.
Child (infers): I may be a good worker, but it's taken me all morning to mow the front lawn. I couldn't be the best worker in the world.

Praise Efforts and Accomplishments— Not Character

On the other hand, when we praise our children's efforts and accomplishments, rather than their character, we free them to make positive inferences about themselves. Praise given in this way, genuinely increases our children's self-esteem. Consider the following examples:

Jessica, age four, had put together a challenging wooden puzzle, which she showed to her mother with pride.

Mother: Did you do it all by yourself?

Jessica: Yes.

Mother: That was a puzzle for a child six to eight-years-old. It must have been hard.

Jessica (fairly bursting with pride): Yes it was, but I did it.

Mother: I can see that I need to get puzzles for you that say up in the corner, "age six to eight, not four to six"!

Jessica: You sure do, because I can do *hard* things.

Mother's praise was effective because she commented on Jessica's *efforts* in putting together a complicated puzzle. Then, Jessica drew her *own* conclusions about her abilities.

As another example, fourteen-year-old Jane had just cleaned up after the "tornado" which had struck her room during the previous week.

Mother: I'm impressed! You cleaned up your room up in one afternoon. What a lot of work to get done. (Comments on child's behavior)

Jane: I even got under the bed.

Mother: What a huge job!

Jane: It sure was! I'm exhausted.

Mother: This room is so clean now it is a pleasure for me to be in here. (Mother describes specifically how a clean room makes her feel).

Jane (infers): I can take on a big job and finish it in an afternoon. I must be quite capable.

As our children rehearse these positive statements over and over in their minds, they enhance their feelings of self-worth.

Validate— Don't Manipulate

Whenever we use praise as a bribe to produce a certain behavior from our children, we unwittingly teach insincerity. We also teach them to be manipulative. Praise used in this way is dangerous medicine because it makes a child feel angry, frustrated, and used. Here are some examples of manipulative praise:

Mother: You're the best baby sitter in the whole city. You also have fabulous taste when it comes to decorating anything. Please change the baby, and let's bring her along to some garage sales. We might even find the desk chair that you've been wanting for your room.

Lisa (age fifteen, infers): I'm not the best baby sitter in the city. I sometimes lose patience and I let my little sister sit in a wet diaper a long time. Mom knows that. She's just trying to get me to tend while she looks around for furniture at garage sales. I have pretty good taste, but it's not fabulous. Mom would never ask me to decorate the living room. She's just being phony. (Mother's praise is so exaggerated and general that Lisa feels it is insincere and she must deny part of it.)

In contrast, sincere praise sounds like this:

Mother: Lisa, this past week I've been so involved in final rehearsals for the MIA dance festival, that I felt overwhelmed.

61

When you picked up your crying baby sister, changed her, fed her applesauce, and entertained her with finger plays, I felt so grateful for your help. Thanks so much. (Mother comments on Lisa's specific behavior and the way it made her feel.) I heard you say you needed a desk chair for your room. I'd surely like to hit the garage sales with you and see what we can find.

Lisa (infers): I'm a helpful person. I'm sensitive to my little sister's needs, and the things I did really helped Mom out of a tight squeeze. When I'm helpful to her, Mom likes to help me with my needs.

Effective praise powerfully communicates acceptance to our children because it isn't used as a tool to get them to do something we want them to do. Rather, it teaches our children sincerity and how it feels to be genuinely valued.

We build meaningful friendships with our children by using praise effectively. Praise is a life-sustaining emotional medicine when we administer it carefully. Try using some of these praise prescriptions:

1. Tuck love notes in gym socks, tennis bags, shirt or skirt pockets, or lunch bags. One daughter wrote: "I'll never forget the day I was in a play at school and Mom couldn't be there because she was sick. I was very disappointed, but when I opened my lunch box and found a bunch of fresh daisies for my hair, I cried. I can still see those fresh flowers from her garden wrapped in a damp cloth with the limp note: 'I'll live every moment on stage with you. You have a way of getting into the character you're playing, and into the heart of the audience. I love you and wish I could be there.'"

2. Add, "It's not like you," to a phrase when a child is honestly not behaving like himself. For example, "It's not like you to be moody. It's not like you at all." This technique turns what could become a criticism into a compliment. If a child is not usually moody, he infers that he must display a sunny

attitude *most* of the time.

3. Try writing notes of commendation on the papers your child brings home from school. Include phrases like, "I like your thinking in this paragraph," "I'd like to see you expand this idea," "I appreciate the wording you used on this page," etc.

4. Develop a list of ways to say "very good" to your children when they perform any task well. They might include: "I like that idea," "I haven't thought of that in quite that way," "You have a way of making me feel happy," "I can't imagine how you could learn all that in just one week," etc.

5. Try playing "caught-cha." Catch your children getting to bed on time, hanging up their clothes, or parking the bicycles properly. Then compliment them: "I feel happy about a tidy closet," or "Finding the bicycles in the bike rack makes me feel like we have an organized home. It must have been a job putting them all away."

6. Give your children a rock-solid compliment when they reach a goal they've been working on. One mother explains, "Through the years, when my children have reached a goal they've been working on or performed well in public, I've given them an unusual rock. I always put the rock in their hand, fold their fingers firmly around it, and say, 'Good job. You've reached a milestone.' We have a jar full of multi-colored stones that recognize various achievements."

It is comforting to know that when we learn to praise effectively we are adding immeasurably to our friendship with our children. We build their self-esteem and enhance their achievements while building emotional bridges.

Unconditional love coupled with sincere praise enlarges the soul. This is the kind of love Sancho offered to the mad knight, Don Quixote, in the musical *The Man of La Mancha*. Sancho loved the old knight, even though he was out of touch with reality, dreamed impractical dreams about making worldly conquests, bestowed his affections on a harlot, and involved Sancho in the details of his incredible quest. Yet, in spite of all this, Sancho sang the endearing phrases, "I like him. I really like him."

With love unfeigned, we can join Sancho in singing the praises of our children, simply because we like them so very, *very* much. As we do so, we reflect part of the gratitude we feel toward Heavenly Father for the miracle of each child.

Befriending the Less Valiant Child

"A mother's unqualified love approaches Christlike love."
—President Ezra Taft Benson

*C*laudia recalls: One day, six-year-old Rachel noticed an almost endless line of automobiles on the freeway. She remarked, "Look at all of those cars. I think they're having a traffic jam, so they're stopping to figure it out."

Often, we mothers find ourselves in a jam, and we need to stop and figure out how we can best influence our children for good. Since much of their time is under the control of school, neighbors, and peers, we often wonder if our efforts have much effect. However, Dr. Ross Campbell states, "Every study I've read indicates that the home wins hands down in every case. The influence of parents far outweighs everything else" (*How To Really Love Your Child*, Wheaton, IL: Victor Books, 1977, p. 16).

Building friendships with our children is one of the best ways to motivate them for good. Ultimately, it may be the most effective way to encourage them to adopt positive values. "In order for a child to identify with his mother or relate closely with her and be able to accept her standards, he must feel genuinely loved and accepted by her," continues Dr. Campbell (p. 137).

Our children are much like a solar music box which has no winding stem. This kind of music box runs by light energy. As light strikes the solar cells in its transparent top, the music box begins to play. Our unconditional love is similar to the solar energy which activates the music box. Dr. Lindsay Curtis, an LDS physician, says, "Every child of God has within his soul the cells that respond to the Light of Christ. His soul has the making of a marvelous music box. A mother's love can help that child eventually permit the Light of Christ to focus upon the music box of his soul" (*Each Child a Challenge*, Salt Lake City, UT: Bookcraft, 1983, p. 83).

Sometimes, however, despite our best efforts, our children are wayward. Sorrow fills our souls like a vulture and its wing-span feels enormous. Even during these times, our impact as mothers is greater than any other, especially when our friendship is genuine. As we reach out and mingle our tears with theirs, we continue to bind them to us. President Joseph F. Smith encourages us to:

> get down and weep with them if necessary and get them to feel tenderly toward you. Use no lash and no violence...
> Approach them with reason, with persuasion and with love unfeigned. With these means, if you cannot gain your boys and your girls...there will be no means left in the world by which you can win them to yourselves. (*Gospel Doctrine*, Salt Lake City, UT: Deseret Book, 1966, p. 316)

In spite of rebellious periods, when our relationship is positive, our children often return to the standards we have taught. President Kimball reassures us:

> I have sometimes seen children of good families rebel, resist, stray, sin, and actually fight God. But I have repeatedly seen many of these same children, after many years of wandering, mellow, realize what they have been missing, repent, and make a great contribution to the spiritual life of their community. The reason I believe this can take place is that, despite all the adverse winds to which these people have been subjected, they have been influenced still more, and much more than they realized, by the current of life in the homes in which they were reared. (*Ensign*, Nov. 1974, p. 111)

One young woman said, "I tried with all my heart, with every fiber of my being, to give up the gospel principles. They were a nuisance to me. I just couldn't do it. I couldn't live with an outraged conscience. I had to bring my way of living in line with the values I had always been taught." With appropriate tolerance and confidence, we mothers may continue to befriend our less valiant children, knowing that we have "motive power" beyond almost any other influence.

Orson Whitney gives a precious promise to every mother whose heart is full of anxiety and whose eyes are filled with tears:

> The Prophet Joseph Smith declared—and he never taught a more comforting doctrine—that the eternal sealings of faithful parents and the divine promises made to them for valiant service in the cause of truth, would save not only themselves but likewise their posterity. Though some of the sheep may wander, the eye of the shepherd is upon them, and sooner or later they will feel the tentacles of Divine Providence reaching out after them and drawing them back to the fold. Either in this life or the life to come, they will return... Pray for your careless and disobedient children. Hold on to them with your faith. Hope on, trust on, till you see the salvation of God. (Conf. Report, April 1929, p. 110-111)

Until that blessed day comes, each mother may bond to her child in friendship and wait patiently and confidently upon that promise and upon the Lord.

President Ezra Taft Benson affirms that building friendships with our children is so vital that their very salvation and eventual exaltation depends on it. He says:

> A child needs a mother more than all the things money can buy. Spending time with your children is the greatest gift of all... God bless you wonderful mothers. We pray for you. We sustain you. We honor you as you bear, nourish, teach, and love for eternity. I promise you the blessings of heaven and all that the Father has as you magnify the noblest calling of all—a mother in Zion. ("To the Mothers in Zion," p. 13)

Let Them Follow Their Own Flight Plan

"The key is love."
—President Ezra Taft Benson

*A*s a mother-daughter team, we are convinced from our own experiences that friendship-building principles underlie meaningful relationships with children of any age. Our personal friendship has deepened as we've exchanged and applied these principles during the sunny and rainy periods of our lives. Many of the ideas we've shared have helped us laugh through our cloudy days and reach out to discover something of the sunshine of genuine love.

As we have written this book together, we have experienced deep satisfaction in listening "heart to heart" as we have discussed changing parenting principles and a mother's unchanging love. In times of discouragement when we have felt desperate for honest praise, we have practiced giving it! A note attached to the "Warm Fuzzy" chapter read, "It's completed! Feel the squeezes sandwiched in between the lines?"

We have each regularly searched the depths of our hearts and the perimeters of our understanding to discover how to show each other as well as our children that our love is unconditional. We have found we can love our children best by becoming genuine friends with them. This is done by accepting them for what they are right now, rather than for what we want them to become. Although unconditional love is an ideal and may be impossible to demonstrate all the time, the closer we come to loving our children that way, the more they are liberated to find themselves.

Dorothy says: Before Stan had graduated from high school he had made a demanding career choice. In fact, he even had a time line pinned above his study desk, detailing the steps leading toward his medical degree.

When he accepted early admission to the university before his senior year, I marvelled at his determination and felt obvious pride. Stan could do it because he had both the brains and the fortitude. I was completely behind him. After his mission, I agonized with him as he tackled chemistry, calculus, and anatomy, steadily progressing toward his goal. Eventually, he graduated with honors from the university, and we decided to go out to lunch and celebrate his efforts.

As we sat down, I asked Stan how he felt about things now that he was so close to applying for medical school. His response was unexpected.

"Well," he began, "I'm not as excited as I thought I'd be."

"Tell me more," I said, encouraging him to talk.

"Well, I keep thinking about when I was a missionary in Spain. At night, I would lie in my bed and listen to the big planes roar overhead. Hearing one, I'd jump up and watch the flashing lights until they disappeared into the blackness. On diversion day, I'd go down to the base in Rota and watch the big ones take off. Sometimes I'd imagine myself trying to pilot one of those big beauties and lift it off the ground."

Noting the animation in his face, I questioned, "It sounds to me like you're feeling drawn to a cockpit instead of a hospital. Is that right?"

"Yeah, Mom, I think I am. I've always loved tinkering with machines. Even when I was a little kid I wanted to make my own hot rod, remember?"

"I do." I admitted. "I guess I thought you'd shifted your interest a little to human machines. I've certainly watched you study enough physiology to make me believe you love it."

"You've gotta understand, Mom. I've tried hard to like medicine, but I can't even pop a water blister without cringing. Last summer, when I worked in the O.R. as a scrub tech, I got nauseated and felt

69

faint when I even smelled the blood."

"I think I'm getting it, Stan," I said as I picked at my salad. "You've decided to change directions, so we're celebrating not only your high marks at the university but your high hopes for a career in the sky, right?"

"Yeah, Mom, I keep thinking about those planes in Rota with me in front of the panel." Three weeks later, Stan arrived at aviation officer candidate school, aspiring to be a navy pilot.

I had gotten in touch with his feelings. Now I had to understand and deal with my own. It had been easy to support my son in his initial career choice because it was familiar. In fact, Stan would have finished his residency about the time his father was ready to take on a partner. I had even envisioned the sign on the door: NIELSEN and NIELSEN. This new venture was different and frightening. Stan wrote of rigorous training sessions in simulators, being shot out of cages into the water, and rehearsing the details of intricate instrument panels. It was all mind-boggling to me.

Eventually, I looked on as the red carpet rolled out to receive my white-uniformed son. The Navy band played "Anchors Away" as he was commissioned an officer. I was impressed, but my heart wasn't soaring. I felt as if I were playing out a script that somebody had reworked with an ending that had come out wrong. Stan should have been choosing a medical specialty, not preparing for his cross-country training flight.

Soon, I stood on the runway with purple, inflated balloons. It was the day he was to circle and touch down on his training flight. I was all nerves, watching my leather-jacketed officer emerge from the cockpit. He was all smiles.

"Well, Mom, would you like a tour of my operating room?" he questioned, motioning toward his plane. I joined him as he explained the wonders of aerodynamics, the excitement of high speed air travel, and the glories of the earth from a cloud's perspective. He was ecstatic over his cross-country mission, and I was absorbed in him and his dream of someday receiving his gold wings.

Later, I watched as he took off to return for his flight evaluation.

Suddenly, at about two thousand feet, I distinctly saw the wings of his airplane tip to the right and then to the left. I panicked!

"What's happening?" I questioned the stranger next to me. "Do you think something's gone wrong?"

"Not at all," he replied with a chuckle. "He's waving goodbye."

I lifted my hand to wave toward the disappearing plane and could almost feel Stan's departing kiss on my cheek. "Ensign Stanley Nielsen...airborne." I said out loud. I could no longer wish for him to be in a hospital when he yearned to be in the skies. He was following his own flight plan, and I finally felt able to follow him.

Unconditional love frees our children to grope and ponder, search and seek in different directions from ours—perhaps better directions for them. Then, when they tip their wings and fly away from us, we remain their valued friends.

About the Authors

Dorothy L. Nielsen and Claudia Nielsen Evans are mother and daughter writers who both have a great interest in families. The wisdom they gained as they overcame many challenges in their lives resulted in this book.

Dorothy graduated from Simmons College in Boston with a degree in pre-professional studies. As an author and a lecturer, she has an impressive resume of recognitions, achievements, and publications. As a presenter at workshops and seminars throughout the U.S., including BYU Education Weeks, Womens Conferences, and Youth Conferences, Dorothy has given over 2,000 hours of service. She has been a Relief Society president and a member of the Young Women's General Board. She is a cultured and accomplished woman and the mother of five outstanding children who also have many accomplishments to their credit. She is the wife of Talmage W. Nielsen, a surgeon, and has written tender articles about the quality of their marriage.

Claudia is a freelance writer, mother of four, and a registered nurse. She received her B.A. in English with a minor in German at Brigham Young University where she graduated after the birth of her first child. She went back to school as a single parent when her second child was two, earning her B.S. and R.N. degrees from the University of Utah and graduating magna cum laude. She worked as an operating room nurse to have day shifts so she could be home with her children after school. An active member of the Church, she has served in many positions including Gospel Doctrine teacher She met her present husband Thomas W. Evans, Jr., at a YSI activity. A year after their marriage in the Salt Lake Temple, they became the parents of twins, giving Tom an instant family of four children! They met the challenge and now live in Bellevue, Washington, where Tom works as a professional engineer.